How to Stop Being Abusiv

Step-by-step Guide On How to Stop Being Emotionally and Physically Abusive, and Stop Being Controlling in Relationships to Build Healthy Respectful, Mutually Beneficial Relationships

Introduction

Abuse, whether emotional or physical, breaks relationships. We all want to be happy, feel loved, respected, and valued. Abuse can undermine any efforts you make in your relationship.

Do you think or know that you are abusive?

Have you ever physically assaulted your partner?

Do you think you are emotionally abusive but aren't sure?

Are you a tad bit too controlling in your relationship?

If this feels like you, then let me take this moment to congratulate you. It takes great courage and self-awareness to realize and admit your faults and then commit to taking the necessary action to make things right, which you area—otherwise, you wouldn't be reading this book.

On your quest to make things right, let this book be your guide. It is what you need to get your relationship back on track.

In it, you will find:

- What abuse is and its effects on your relationship
- How to determine if you are abusive

- How to stop being controlling

- Ways to stop physical and emotional abuse

- How to get help for you and your partner

- ***And so much more!***

If you feel like you've lost all hope and control, let this book show you that you haven't.

Let's begin!

PS: I'd like your feedback. If you are happy with this book, please leave a review on Amazon.

Please leave a review for this book on Amazon by visiting the page below:

https://amzn.to/2VMR5qr

Table of Content

Introduction _____ 2

Chapter 1: What Is Abuse? _____ 7

   Types of Abuse in Relationships _____ 9

   Physical Abuse _____ 10

   How To Know If You are Physically Abusive ___ 11

   Emotional Abuse _____ 12

   How To Know If You are Emotionally Abusive   12

Chapter 2: The Primary Cause Of Abusive Behavior (And How to Deal With It) _____ 16

   Dealing with The Root of the Problem _____ 21

   Factors That Can Accelerate Abuse _____ 26

Chapter 3: What Drives Our Need For Control? _____ 34

   Why Is Control Important to You? _____ 35

   How To Let Go Of The Need For Control _____ 37

Chapter 4: How To Stop Being Controlling

(Where to Begin) _____ 41

Admission _____ 41

What to Do _____ 42

After Acceptance _____ 45

Chapter 5: The Big Talk (Admitting Abusiveness To Your Partner) _____ 47

How To Talk to Your Partner _____ 48

Prepare _____ 49

Apologizing and Developing Empathy _____ 51

Making The Actual Apology _____ 53

A Sample Apology for Being Emotionally Abusive _____ 54

Chapter 6: About Knowing Your Triggers (& False Beliefs) _____ 56

What Are Triggers? _____ 57

"We Should Both Feel Bad Together" _____ 59

Your Anger Journal _____ 60

Trigger Solution Suggestions for Different Types Of Abuse _____ 61

Chapter 7: Clear, Open Communication is The Key _____ 67

Learn How To Express Yourself _____ 68

Conclusion_____ 74

Chapter 1: What Is Abuse?

The room was quiet, and I couldn't help but feel rather uncomfortable. Ben and I sat quietly, waiting for Josh to speak. He had called us to his house, sounding rather shaken up.

"It happened again! It was bad, and this time she left," he said with his head down. We already knew what he was going to next,

"I don't know what happened! I don't know what came over me," He blurted out.

Josh and his wife Martha were your typical next-door couple. They fell in love in college, and their honeymoon phase seemed to last forever. They were one of those couples who never kept anything from each other; they would even tell each other what they had for lunch and things like that.

I had only met them a few months after their wedding at a mutual friend's wedding, and I couldn't help but admire how happy they were; they always held hands, whispered little things in each other's ears, and gave each other random kisses. You can understand why I was so surprised when he called me the first time they had a nasty fight over something so trivial: a broken window pane.

One morning after having breakfast, Josh and Martha both frantically prepared themselves to get to work; they had woken up a bit late because, apparently, Martha had forgotten to set the alarm clock.

Martha was rinsing a few dishes on the sink, and Josh had just come in after taking out the trash. As Martha was cleaning the sink, she seemed to notice the windowpane, yet again, and she asked Josh why he hadn't fixed it yet, even after she had told him countless times.

Josh replied by saying that it wasn't the time to be talking about windowpanes as they were already late. However, Martha insisted and told him that they never really talked about anything, and the windowpane was just one more thing he was trying to dodge.

As much as it wasn't the time to be talking about windowpanes, Martha was right; they never really talked about real issues, at least not in a healthy way that builds the relationship.

Before they knew it, hurtful words were flying around, and they got a little bit too close to each other, and it wasn't long before Josh found himself shaking and pushing Martha to the wall. Before he noticed what he had done, Martha was out of the door, gone! I can only tell you that things went downhill from here.

Have you ever encountered such a situation?

Have you ever felt that dark cloud that, when it cleared, leaves destruction behind that you had no intention of creating? Be it words or through action, you are not alone; many people experience this. Fortunately, by understanding abuse, you can make it better.

Types of Abuse in Relationships

There are different types of abuse, but some can manifest into one. Generally, abuse can either be emotional or physical, and both severely impact you and your partner.

Some of the other types of abuse include:

- ***Sexual abuse*:** Yes, there can be sexual abuse in relationships, where you use any form of coercing or pressure to get your partner to do something sexual.

- ***Verbal abuse*:** This involves regular name-calling, cursing, and belittling, which humiliates your partner.

- ***Financial abuse***: This involves controlling your partner's finances or their ability to work.

Most of these come down to emotional and physical abuse

and control issues, which is why we shall focus on that:

Physical Abuse

Physical abuse involves using physical force against your partner. It hurts both you and your partner. If you have been physically abusive before, you know the guilt and hurt you feel upon seeing what you did to your partner. Physical abuse usually starts gradually and then escalates over time.

For Josh and Martha, that shove was the first incident, but the last incident was notably terrible. As we asked him what happened, he was hesitant to speak up or about it. It was as if he didn't believe that he was capable of what he had done. Finally, Ben, being an impatient guy, nudged him to tell us what happened.

"She was on the floor, and I was kicking and kicking! I couldn't seem to stop!" That's all he said. We didn't know what to say either.

With physical abuse, it only gets worse. And so, if you are here after your first incident, then I'm glad you came here in time; again, if not, I'm still glad you are here because it means you are eager to improve yourself, which is a sign of self-awareness and the desire to improve as a person.

Physical abuse can encompass sexual and verbal abuse.

How To Know If You are Physically Abusive

Other than the obvious sign of physically assaulting your partner, you can identify intent and also the action. To get started on that, please answer the following questions as honestly as possible—please be honest with yourself.

- Have you ever raised your hands at your partner?
- Have you ever thought about raising your hand at your partner?
- What do you do when you feel outraged?
- Have you ever engaged in a fight with a friend or someone you know because you were angry?
- Do you find yourself punching things and throwing them because you are angry?
- Have you ever been arrested for violence in one form or the other?
- Has someone ever told you that you are abusive?
- Do you feel that your partner is afraid of you?

If you've answered yes to most of these questions, then there is a high chance that you are physically abusive to your partner. Let's look at emotional abuse briefly before we dive into why you might be abusive.

Emotional Abuse

When people hear of emotional abuse, they usually think about a person saying mean things to their partner. While that is part of it, unfortunately, it goes deeper and way beyond that. Emotional abuse also involves using emotions to blame, criticize or shame the other person.

Let's dive a little into it so that you can understand if you are emotionally abusive.

How To Know If You are Emotionally Abusive

Emotional abuse can include the following:

- **Rejection:** Rejecting your partner's opinions, thoughts, or ideas
- **Verbal abuse:** Swearing at your partner and yelling
- **Gaslighting**: Twisting or manipulating the truth
- **Threats:** Threatening your partner and intimidating them
- **Put-downs:** Public embarrassment, calling

names/telling your partner they are stupid

- **Silent treatment:** Where you suddenly stop talking to your partner without telling them why
- **Isolating:** Limiting movement or stopping your partner from contacting other people or doing certain activities like sports.

Emotional abuse can also include financial abuse.

To help you know if you are generally abusive, I would like to narrow it down and use the **ICJ strategy**.

Please take a moment to identify if you portray any of the following traits in your relationship:

I: Isolate

Do you feel that your partner shouldn't spend time with or around people other than you? How do you feel when your partner is out with other people?

If you notice that your partner is going out less often than they did before, or if they have fewer friends than before, then maybe you are abusive.

C: Control

Do you feel like you need to control everything your partner does? Do you feel like your way should be the only way in the relationship? Do you text or call your spouse many times when they go somewhere without you?

If it seems like things are always done your way in a relationship or that your partner never gets a say in things, then you are likely controlling. Additionally, if you also assume that something concerning both of you should happen your way and you don't need to consult your partner before doing it, you are probably controlling.

J: Jealousy

A bit of jealousy in a relationship is healthy and normal. After all, nobody wants their partner to spend a considerable amount of time with an ex or constantly text or talk about a particular person. However, a problem develops when jealousy becomes too much and sometimes unreasonable.

If you constantly feel paranoid and want to know where your partner is and what they are doing all the time, then there might be a problem. If you find yourself constantly checking your partner's phone or going further and tracking their phone, there is a *huge* problem.

As you will see later, being this controlling and jealous often stems from an underlying Let's look at this in the next chapter.

Chapter 2: The Primary Cause Of Abusive Behavior (And How to Deal With It)

Every behavior, yes, every single one, is explainable, and if you dig deep enough, you can work your way back to the roots of any action.

Certainly, you didn't wake up one day and decide to start abusing your partner(s); nothing can be further from the truth. Can you recall when it all started? What were the circumstances at that time? Had anything significant happened to you? How were your past relationships?

The truth of the matter is that most abusers have been victims of abuse themselves. Behind abuse lies a certain fear; it could be a fear that you don't want to lose your partner; you need them and want them to be in your life. That is certainly a good thing, but when it comes out as abuse, problems begin.

However, the bigger problem is that most abusers never realize their level of abuse nor recognize it as abuse. Why is this?

The most probable reason for this is that you have probably experienced similar abuse, and now, you recognize it as normal. Because your mind interpreted that abuse as normal, you believe your actions are rational when they are borderline abusive. This especially applies to emotional abuse but can sometimes apply to physical abuse.

So when this becomes 'normal,' it becomes challenging to acknowledge your abusiveness towards your partner. That is part of why it is so wonderful that you are here: you have recognized that something is not right—congrats again! It takes a lot of courage and insight.

Your childhood

Our childhood sets the foundation of who we become as adults; this is why the childhood stage is so important. Being abusive can all come down to your childhood.

If you dealt with or observed physical abuse as a child, you are more likely to become abusive when you grow up. Likewise, if you lost control somewhere along the way as you grew up, you are likelier to become more controlling as an adult.

Now that I've mentioned that, I remember a conversation Josh and I had before his first incident with Martha. We were having dinner over a few drinks, and we were talking about our past lives. Josh was more on the quiet side, and he never really liked sharing. However, after a few beers, he was a talker.

His parents got divorced when he was 17, and believe it or not, that was the highlight of his childhood. Before this, his house was a warzone. According to him, no single day passed without his parents fighting, be it physically or throwing words at each other. Sometimes they would go a month without uttering a word to each other.

In such circumstances, Josh had to be the middleman. If his mother wanted something from his dad, she would have him ask for it and vice versa. After their divorce, he went on to live with his mom. A few months later, his mother got a new boyfriend, and even within a few months, they were already fighting.

Josh could swear on his life that the very first time they fought, his mother had prompted the fight. According to him, his mom and her new boyfriend were arguing as ordinary people do, and out of nowhere, she slapped and shoved her new man, and that's where it began.

You see, for someone like Josh's mom, this behavior had become her new normal. Because of exposure to it for decades, she had accepted that the best way to deal with arguments was through physical means.

On the other hand, Joshdetested it when things got physical;

he loathed it! That is why he was always so shaken up after every incident with Martha. He would always say, *"I can't become like my parents. I know I'm better than this!"* And yet, he would perpetuate the behavior repeatedly.

It wasn't just physical, though. When Martha had told him that they never really talked about anything, she meant the silent treatment that ensued after arguments. Unlike his parents, they wouldn't stay months without talking to each other, but they would sometimes not talk for weeks after an argument. Josh's relationship was slowly turning out like that of his parents. He saw it, but he felt as if he had no control over it.

What does this mean?

Like Josh, all this means you are not a bad person, and we can explain away your abusive behavior.

Look back at your childhood and be honest with yourself. Unfortunately, people who have experienced abuse—of any kind—tend to bury it deep inside them because they often struggle to face what they experienced.

Ask yourself these questions and answer them as honestly as you can:

- Did you have a smooth childhood?

- Were there cases of abuse (physical or emotional) between your parents/guardians?

- Has a person in authority ever abused you?

- In what kind of environment/neighborhood did you grow up? Were cases of abuse a regular thing?

- How was your relationship with your parents/guardians? Did any of them ever abuse you?

- How is your relationship with your parents now? Has anything changed?

Don't be afraid to dig as deep as you need to dig and remind yourself of your goal. If you don't deal with your past trauma, you will struggle to change and improve your relationship. No matter how hard it might be to dig into childhood memories, doing this for yourself will make all the difference.

Exercise

Go the old-fashioned way and take a pen and paper. Hold the pen in your hands as you think far back. Try and link your actions to something from your past. If it is anger, feel it; if you feel sad, feel it but don't bury it inside.

Write down why you think you are abusive now. Come up with one particular incident from what you just wrote and be as detailed as you can. Then, come up with another incident from your present where you were being abusive and then compare the two situations.

How different or similar are the situations? Have you found your root cause? I would like to believe so.

Dealing with The Root of the Problem

Assuming that you have dug deep into your childhood and you've seen where everything might have stemmed from, it is now time to deal with it.

NOTE: I feel the need to mention that I'm not a certified therapist. However, I have dealt with abuse myself, and I am well-read and have helped many people in my circle deal with their problems and make their relationships better. Josh is one such person that I helped, and believe it or not, he and his partner are now happily married and expecting their third child—but we will get into this later.

Now, consider the following statements:

"Where are you? Did you go out? Are you cheating on me?

"I need to know where you are all the time."

"I don't want you seeing your friends all the time."

Have you ever uttered any of these statements or similar ones to your partner? If you can relate, read on. Let's dig a bit deeper into the first statement.

True, your concerns might be legitimate but let's get your partner out of the picture for a minute and focus on you and your concerns.

Regardless of where your partner is or what they are doing, consider answering the following:

- Why are you so concerned about where your partner is?

- Why do you think that they are cheating?

- Do you believe that they are cheating, or are you just fearful that they might?

- What about your partner makes you believe that they are out cheating?

- Did they do or say something to suggest this?

As you answer these questions, try to be as unbiased as you can. In other words, think from a logical point of view: no feelings or anger attached.

When it comes down to it, you will realize that all of these statements come from fear. You have no problem with your spouse going out, but you are afraid that they may cheat and you might lose them.

You may have no problem with your partner spending time with friends, but you might have a problem with one of her friends with whom you believe your partner might cheat or influence them to do the same. The point here is, deep down, you know that your partner can't cheat on you, but your fear clouds that judgment.

Do this instead

The trick here is to **pause** and **think**: whenever such a thought comes into mind, literally stop in your tracks. Ask yourself, "Where is this thought coming from?' Then, face the thought with logic.

For instance, let's say your partner got mugged coming home from a place you told her not to go. So they come home, feeling scared and shaken up, and they tell you what happened. If your mind tells you to say something like, "I told you so, you deserve what happened to you," stop and think:

Does my partner truly deserve it?

Couldn't it have happened to anyone?

Is it my partner's fault that the mugger chose to mug them?

Aren't you glad that they didn't injure, or worse, kill your partner?

When you answer these questions deeply and honestly, you will realize that your statement is utterly unfair, and you will have something nicer and more comforting to say.

What about physical abuse?

The same applies to physical abuse but in a different way.

Emotions are very unreliable. When we feel outraged, our voice of logic disappears from our brains; it is like it never existed. That is why you can do or say hurtful things that you later come to regret. In some cases, you might not even remember saying or doing some things.

Has this ever happened to you? Well, it happens to most of us.

The trick here is to notice when things are about to escalate. You can always tell when things are about to get out of control; you can always feel it. Unfortunately, it is tricky to get out of this state when things have already gone out of control. Therefore, the best thing you can do is learn to read the room and identify when things are about to spiral.

Some of the signs to look out for include:

- Extreme raising of voices

- Spewing hate towards your partner or cursing

- Increased breathing and sometimes shaking and sweating

- Almost seeing blurry (but it shouldn't get to this point because, at this point, you are probably too far gone)

- Your partner telling you to calm down or you will do something you will regret (always listen to this cue)

When you experience any of the above, make a hasty retreat. Doing this will require you to muster a lot of self-control because it can be hard to do, especially if you are already too far gone.

All you need do is tell your partner that you need to leave, and you will continue the conversation when you have both calmed down a little. If your partner continues pressuring you to finish the conversation, let them know that it is impossible and you don't want to hurt them. Telling your partner this will give them the cue to let things go for the moment.

Factors That Can Accelerate Abuse

As you learn more about abusive behavior, you also need to learn about factors that can make you more abusive and heighten abuse incidences. These factors include:

Alcohol and drug use

While I'm not a qualified expert, I can tell you that alcohol makes any anger you may be feeling 100 times worse than it actually is. Drugs alter how we think and behave; some drugs can make you mellow while others can make you hyper.

You are the only one who knows how particular drugs affect you; therefore, you have to be very aware of this. Things worsen if you are a chronic drug user, and therefore, if you are, you need to get some professional help.

In other words, if you get abusive after drinking or using other drugs and do this often, the first thing you will need to do is get drug use help, then focus on the abuse after rehab. You might be surprised to find out that you never abuse your partner when you are sober.

Stress

Stress can also be a factor that worsens abuse.

Have you ever been immensely stressed? How did that feel? Have you ever done something you regretted because you were so stressed?

Well, it's because stress pressure can be too much, and you might take it out on your partner. While it might not be right, it does happen. In this case, you need to find healthy ways of dealing with stress and releasing it. Keeping things bottled up is your number one enemy because the bottle will fill up at some point, and when it does, it will blow.

Find someone to talk to; it could be your partner, friend, or anyone else you trust: find a release channel for your mind.

You could also try other stress management techniques such as:

Meditation

There are many forms of meditation you can try. You don't need to employ meditation only when you feel overwhelmed; you can make it part of your lifestyle to make its practice easier.

Here is a basic meditation procedure for stress-relief:

- **Get Comfortable:** Select where and how you will position yourself as you meditate. Most people prefer a comfy chair, while others prefer sitting cross-legged on the ground—not on the bare ground, though; find a soft cushion or carpet so that you can be fully comfortable. However, avoid laying down because it can get so relaxing that you end up sleeping. Keep your back straight, and don't let your shoulders slump; if they do as you meditate, straighten back up.

- **Slowly Close Your Eyes:** Once in position, adopt a soft gaze, look into the distance, and slowly lower your eyelids. Your jaw should remain slightly open and slack—ensure that you relax all your facial muscles. If your face tightens, open your eyes slowly and refocus a soft gaze and lower again.

NOTE: Don't tightly squeeze your eyes; instead, close them softly and naturally, as if you were asleep. At this point, relaxing your whole body is the aim. Assess every part of yourself and if you feel any tension, focus on that part, breathe deeply into it and let your breath relax you.

- **Thoughts Aside:** While it is impossible to control thoughts, it is possible to control the power they have over you. Don't get me wrong; this does not mean you should suppress or ignore your thoughts or the feelings they stir up. It simply means you can choose to remain calm, note them, and breathe deeply to bring yourself back into the moment. Learning this technique in meditation will also help you apply it in real life, where you can easily let things go. Letting go is essential for stress management; after all, sometimes, we get stressed because we forget that we cannot control everything.

- **Proceed:** That is it: all there is to it is to recognize distracting thoughts that may pop up and put them aside to keep your mind clear and at peace.

Getting adequate sleep

Have you ever been extra irritated because you didn't get enough sleep? I have been there myself and know many other people who can relate to this too.

When we sleep, we allow our bodies to rest and reset. Your brain takes this time to process the day's events, store memories, and make room for new lessons and ideas. If you don't get enough sleep, it interrupts this process, which can impact your mood.

To ensure you get enough sleep, you can use the following tips:

- Have a constant sleep and wake up time. When you teach your body how to wake up and sleep at a particular time, it normalizes your body's circadian rhythm. The circadian rhythm is your body's natural wake and sleep cycle. Ensure you set your alarm for when you wake up and make sure you are in bed 30 minutes before your actual bedtime. Exposure to bright, natural light during the day is another great way to reset your circadian rhythm.

- Keep electronic devices away from the bedroom at least an hour or two before your bedtime. We all know how distracting our phones can be, thanks to the breadth of things we can do on that tiny device. If you struggle with getting enough sleep mainly because of this, consider putting your phone in another room for the night.

- Do not have heavy meals right before bed, and ensure you eat enough before going to bed. Sleeping on a full, stretched stomach is uncomfortable, and you might even fall asleep; on the other hand, sleeping on an empty stomach is difficult; the key here is moderation.

- Avoid caffeine and other stimulates in the evening. Coffee makes you alert, and you don't want to be alert come bedtime.

- You can also optimize your bedroom to make it as comfortable as possible. For example, have dim lights, play relaxing sounds that can help you sleep, etc.

Getting enough sleep will help you be more relaxed. When you eliminate the irritation that comes with a lack of adequate sleep, you will listen more—conversely, you will also be more understanding.

Journaling

Any approach that helps you release your thoughts is an excellent way to relieve stress. Journaling is one such way. The good thing about journaling is that you don't have to worry about people judging you: you can write anything that comes into your mind.

Get yourself a journal and pen, and then pen down anything bothering you. Write whatever you feel and be as detailed as possible. You can divide your thoughts into columns. For example:

Thought	Feeling	Reasoning	Solution
1.			

In the reasoning section, try your best to describe why you might be feeling what you are feeling. For the solution, write about something you think you can do to feel better and then do it.

Physical Activity

Did you know that when you exercise, the body releases dopamine, a feel-good hormone? Many forms of physical activity lead to the production of dopamine. That's why you will see people in movies—and real-life—going for a jog when they feel overwhelmed.

Again, here you don't need to engage in physical activity only when you feel stressed. You can make it part of your lifestyle to ensure you get a daily dose of dopamine and feel better about yourself every day. Besides, exercising is a great way to keep in shape. However, if you feel stressed and need release right away, go ahead and run or go to the gym.

NOTE: If you feel super stressed, do your best to avoid any heated arguments with your partner until you feel better. If one ensues, walk away. Compared to your partner being angry because of abusive behavior, being angry because you walked away is the lesser of two evils.

When you get back, calmly talk to your partner about the feelings that prompted you to walk away. I guarantee that if your partner loves you and values the relationship, understanding is the only thing you will get.

The need for control is another primary cause of abusiveness In relationships. Let's focus on it.

Chapter 3: What Drives Our Need For Control?

As mentioned, the need for control is one of the core causes of many forms of abuse. For example:

- You can be verbally abusive because you want your partner to do things a certain way that your partner doesn't agree with for this or that reason. When they disagree with you, verbal abuse ensues.

- You can be physically abusive because your partner won't let an issue go while you don't want to continue arguing. The need to stop the argument (and control things) can be so intense that you raise your hand and strike your partner.

- You can be financially abusive because you want money spent a certain way, and when your partner goes against this, you feel like you have lost control and turn to abusiveness.

The point is, control is a significant part of being abusive. Fortunately, if you learn how to let go of control, things will be much easier for you.

However, if you've tried it before, you know that letting go is easier said than done. So, before we look at how you can let go of control, let's look into why we want to be in control.

Why Is Control Important to You?

Again, a healthy degree of control is good; it keeps things in order. The problem develops when the desire to control things becomes so much that you can do anything, including being abusive, to attain it.

You see, everything comes down to our childhood. Most people who feel they lost control when they were younger tend to be overly controlling. For instance, if your parents or guardians dictated—and still dictate—what you should do with your life, who's good for you and who is not, etc., you will project this onto someone else, usually your partner. In most cases, you do this to regain some of the control you lost as a child.

However, it can also be the other way round where people always offloaded their responsibilities to you, so you always needed to step up.

For example, if you come from a single-parent household, especially one where there were drug use issues, and you always had to step up and keep the house running, you are likely to be very controlling. When other people are incapable or feign incapability towards you, especially people supposed to be in authority, you can start feeling and thinking people are incapable and need someone to control them.

Beyond that, control is also a part of some fear or anxiety. Some people try to control others to fall into a predictable pattern such that there are no surprises or deviations from their expected results.

Such people may feel that if things happen or get done how they want it and when they want it, there will be less disruption. Unfortunately, that is not the case. You can't control a human being, especially a grown person. Whatever efforts you make to do that will meet resistance that will trigger abusive behavior. That calls to mind an important question:

Is it the other person's fault for failing to do something they don't entirely agree with, or are you at fault? You may argue yes, but remember that everyone, even someone married to you.

Please answer these questions as honestly as you can:

- Do you feel any of the sentiments expressed above?
- Do you feel that you need your partner to do whatever you want, no questions asked?
- Do you feel like if your partner does something that

deviates from your 'plans,' things won't go well?

- Do you get outraged when your partner disagrees with you?

- Do you feel that you need to do certain things to make sure that your partner loves you forever?

If YES is your answer to most of these questions, then you have control issues that you need to work on and let go off:

How To Let Go Of The Need For Control

First, you have to let your partner love you the way they want to love you. You can't force your partner to love you a certain way. Partnerships are much sweeter when things flow; when you force things, you will feel the strain on your relationship.

How would you feel if your partner said you could not spend time with certain friends or if your partner told you to choose between them and your work? You would feel bad because nobody wants to live in another person's shadow.

Here are some key things you can do to stop being controlling:

Learn about anxiety

Instead of using control as a defense mechanism against feeling uncertain, assess every detail of the fear that drives you into controlling your partner.

Is it the fear of losing them? The fear of cheating? The fear of being vulnerable to them or needing them too much?

Whatever it is, read books about it or even consult a therapist. The more you know, the easier it shall be to identify any self-sabotaging behaviors and determine which healthier ones you can use as replacements.

Assess the effectiveness of your efforts

As you consider how you can stop being controlling, ask yourself if controlling your partner makes any lasting difference or if it just brings undesirable effects.

For instance, if you are trying to get your partner to quit her job, ask yourself how intervening helps. Does your partner work for an abusive boss and now wants to quit that working environment? If so, by all means, keep pushing. However, if your partner loves her job and you only want her to quit for your reasons, how will your need to exert control affect the relationship?

In this example, the chances are high that your partner

doesn't want to quit, and pressuring her might even mean the end of your relationship. If your efforts to control don't bring any value to your partner, reconsider your actions.

See things from a different perspective

Sometimes all it takes is support from the right person. Instead of relying on your efforts only, seek support from a close friend (or therapist). Ask them if they think you are controlling, and let them tell you exactly how.

You can even ask the person what they think you should do to be less controlling; you might be surprised at the suggestions you get. Doing this will help you identify and work on unconscious behaviors that may be stemming from your issues.

Don't 'Speak' Control

To become less controlling, you need to understand the role your language plays. Think about the language you use to exercise control. For instance, let's say your partner asks you if you like her outfit. Here, your control language could be something like, "Can you try and wear something less revealing."

If this is your regular control language, your replies would sound something like, *can you not do that now, or can you do this...*, *etc.* The point here is that there are certain words you use when exercising control; there is also a particular tone that you use. Recognize both and do your best to avoid them as much as possible.

If you find yourself using the controlling tone or controlling words, be aware enough to recognize this—meditation should help with awareness—and rephrase your statement into something that will help your partner instead of hurting them.

I know that this will be a bit hard, and you will experience many slip-ups, but go out of your way to commend yourself for all the times you manage to let go of control. This process takes time, but if you remain committed to it, you will get there.

Let's take things a step further:

Chapter 4: How To Stop Being Controlling (Where to Begin)

At this point, you have learned a lot, and you are probably eager to start your journey towards healing. If you are wondering where to start, here it is:

Admission

As Josh described to us the last incident between him and his wife, I still hadn't heard him admit to being abusive even though he was mortified by what he did. He kept saying that he didn't want to be like his parents or that his wife would never return to him after the last incident, but I heard no admittance to any wrongdoing.

I stopped him in his tracks and asked him, "You know that you are abusive to your partner, right?" Josh retracted and said, "I'm not abusive per se; it's just this anger and the stress we are both going through because of the mortgage. And then Martha keeps saying these things..." and he kept going on about the things not going right in his life then.

Every time he would call us and tell us what happened, he never admitted to being abusive to his wife, and I was sure to mention it this time around. I asked him why it was so difficult to admit that he was abusive even though it was very clear. He simply said, "I don't want to be abusive. I don't want to be one of those men referred to as women beaters." I quietly said, "But you are."

What followed was a long minute of silence. He didn't say anything for one or two entire minutes; he just looked down at his beer. I only noticed the streams of tears from his eyes because I could see them going right into his bottle. My husband comforted him as he broke down and repeated that he was abusive and he was so sorry to Martha. That was the night that everything changed. He has never touched Martha abusively from that night.

I believe that if Josh never faced up to his abusiveness, things would now have changed. Knowing that you hit or emotionally abuse your partner is one thing, but coming out clean to yourself is an entirely different thing.

That's why you need to admit it to yourself; it makes all the difference:

What to Do

Admitting that you are abusive won't be easy. After all, nobody wants to cop up to emotional or physical abuse, a hurt partner, or a broken relationship. No one wants to know that their behavior has damaged someone they love. While that may be the case, you have to remember that admitting it will get things on the path to betterment; it could even save your relationship.

Unfortunately, even when they know this is true, most abusive and controlling partners often push the truth away and go into denial. Why is this? We can attribute it to human nature riddled with shame and guilt. That means understanding shame and guilt is one of the things you need to do to get started on admitting that you are abusive to your partner.

Shame and guilt

Most people assume that shame and guilt are the same things; they are not.

Experiencing guilt usually comes from the fear of punishment, but when we make amends with the person we hurt or get punished, it resolves the guilt. With shame, we fear abandonment. In other words, we feel shameful for what we are and guilty for what we do. These feelings usually overlap, but guilt can be easier to deal with than shame.

When you feel shame, you can become depressed or e depressed or even suicidal. That happens because sh strips off your fragile self-image and sense of pride.

It's important to remind yourself that it is human to f

therefore, shame can be your first hope towards healing. It shows you that you are now aware that you are failing to become who you desire to be. It can show you parts of yourself that you might have been oblivious to in the past. Self-awareness is often the first step towards growth.

Say it to yourself

Find somewhere quiet where you can think undisturbed. Reflect on the times you have abused your partner and detail out every instance. Think about how your partner felt at that time, i.e., put yourself in their shoes.

Do you think your partner felt degraded, fearful, or terrified? Do you think your partner felt bad about themselves after the abuse? How did the incidences affect your relationship in each case? Did the two of you grow further apart? Did communication between you become worse?

Seeing the impact of your actions can help you see things for what they are, making admittance easier. After the reflection session, finish it by saying the words, "I am abusive." Please don't end it with "buts." Leave it at "I am abusive" to get yourself started on the self-acceptance process.

After Acceptance

After admitting it to yourself, please think about why you are abusive in the first place. If you have any feelings of shame or guilt, remember why you are doing this and that you're not the only one at fault. The past doesn't matter; what you are trying to do here is all that matters—and your partner will be more than happy that you are working on yourself to better and enhance your relationship.

Continue working on any unfinished business from the past so that when you talk to your partner, at least you will be somewhere different.

A good place to start is to assess your anger. While it is easy to get enraged with your spouse, your anger towards the original abuser is possibly still buried deep inside you. As unbelievable as it sounds, this might be the anger you might have been holding on to (even if it was many years ago) that makes you so enraged with your partner. Making this all-important connection is what you need to do to start healing.

Use your current anger to help you access the suppressed anger from your past. Who abused you? What was the nature of the abuse? How did it make you feel then, and how does it make you feel now?

Don't be afraid of the mixture of emotions you might feel. It might be that the very same person who abused you as a child is still in your life, and you laugh and dine together, suppressing your genuine feelings.

If this person isn't still in your life, work with the memories and feel what you need to feel. I know this can be scary, especially if it was someone important in your life, but you need to work past this to move forward.

TIP: If your abuser is still in your life, you might want to hold off confronting this person until you get a hold of your anger. The realization of the anger you feel towards the person may be too intense, and you may end up saying or doing something you might regret.

Chapter 5: The Big Talk (Admitting Abusiveness To Your Partner)

This is where the real work is; if you thought that admitting to yourself that you have been abusive was hard, admitting it to your partner can be harder because, one, you feel shame and guilt, and two, you might lack the courage to face your partner or words to say to communicate how sorry you are. This is especially true if you are reserved and communication is not one of your biggest strengths.

You might also be one of those people who struggle to admit any wrongdoing and instead try to cover up any vulnerability or weakness to appear strong. If any of this is true, don't worry, we shall look at what you can do.

You may be wondering why it is so important to admit it to your partner too. You might argue that since you've admitted it to yourself and are working on it, that's what matters. Well, this isn't true:

First, admitting that you are abusive to your partner is a great step towards fighting denial. Admitting it to your partner makes sure that you never deny it in the future—because it will be out in the open.

Secondly, you owe it to your partner to admit that you have

been abusive, and you know you have. With prolonged emotional abuse especially, it is easy for your partner to start feeling *crazy or as if they are imagining everything happening.*

By failing to take responsibility, your partner may start thinking that it is their fault and that they are the problem. When you own up to your wrongs, you will clear any doubt and confirm their perceptions and feelings. Alone, this can give your partner a considerable sense of relief and hope for a better relationship.

The final reason is that you need to take accountability for your actions. Don't minimize and don't hedge; taking responsibility will be great for your soul and self-respect. It will also show your partner that you have grown and can change for the better; it shows that you have inner resolve.

How To Talk to Your Partner

After Josh broke down that night, he knew what he had to do. He wanted to call Martha right away so that they could talk, but I advised him to wait a while. Martha needed time to calm down and process what had happened. She needed some time alone, and Josh needed the same.

I advised him to take some time to reflect on all the aspects at play. Why he might be abusive, what bothers him the most, what he would tell Martha etc. He admitted that he hadn't thought about that; he just felt that he needed to talk to his wife.

After a week of soul searching, he finally called her. Martha was staying at a friend's, and they hadn't talked at all during that period.

"Hey Hun, could we please talk. Do you think you can hear me out?"

The statement took Martha by surprise a little. Josh had given her the option to hear him out only if she wanted to. Earlier, he would have told her something like, "Please come home. You need to hear me out."

This sole statement is probably the only thing that made Martha go back and give them a chance. Later, Martha confided that she had resolved to divorce him. However, because of this, they had a chance.

That shows just how important it is to frame your statements and apology.

Prepare

First, ensure you are both in a position to communicate and listen to each other openly. You will be pouring out your heart to your partner; therefore, you need to pick a time and place where you can communicate openly, for long, and without any distractions. Yes, your home is the best place to have this conversation, but a quiet restaurant will also work if your partner does not feel comfortable with that.

Secondly, rehearse all aspects of what you will talk about so that you don't deviate. The point of this particular conversation is to be open about your past, admit that you are abusive, and let your partner know that you are on your path to change; the more details you give, the better.

Be Direct

When it comes to the actual conversation, I suggest that you be as straightforward as possible; casually slipping what you need to say into a conversation is not a good idea.

Instead, make your intentions clear by telling your partner that you have something important to talk about or say. Then, once you meet, face your partner, and look them in the eye (if you can). If you find this hard to do, then you can write your partner a letter. Whether it is face to face or through a letter, ensure you include the following in your conversation:

- A precise statement admitting that you have been abusive

- Certain examples of such attitude or behavior

- A statement of remorse and regret for your behavior and an unwavering assurance to continue working on personality or behavior change towards your partner.

Be extra careful not to blame your partner in any way. Avoid statements such as, "I dis ___ because you said_____." Such statements will only show that you are not willing to take accountability for your actions.

Instead, talk to your partner about why you think you are abusive. The more you let your partner in and allow them to see you truly, the better the conversation shall pan out. However, even as you tell your partner why you may think you are abusive, make it clear that you are responsible for your healing and change.

Apologizing and Developing Empathy

After acknowledging your abusiveness to your partner, the next thing you need to do is apologize for that behavior. A sincere heartfelt apology will be healing for both you and your partner.

However, before you voice your apology, you have to develop empathy towards your partner; this is the only way you can give a meaningful apology.

Here is how to get started on that:

- Again, begin by thinking about what your partner felt when you physically or emotionally abused her. Could your partner have been angry, hurt, disappointed, afraid, etc.?

- Now go ahead and ponder on the effects of your behavior on your partner's self-esteem. Do you have an idea of how your actions or words damaged your partner's self-image?

- If you had denied taking responsibility for particular actions, do you know how this would have affected your partner?

- Can you imagine how trapped your partner must have felt if you always tried to dominate or control everything about their life?

- Do you think it was easy for your partner to live with you?

If you are still having a hard time putting yourself in your partner's shoes, don't feel discouraged; keep trying. As you keep working on it, you will get there.

Here are a few pointers:

- Ask your partner to tell you how your actions affected her, and keenly listen to what your partner says.

- Reverse roles and pretend that you are your partner and talk about how the whole thing affected you—do this alone. You can also write from your partner's POV.

Making The Actual Apology

To give a meaningful apology, it must encompass the 3R's: regret, responsibility, and remedy. You have to include all 3R's; otherwise, the other person will feel that something is missing and may even feel as if you are insincere.

Basically:

- **Regret** involves offering a statement of regret for your actions and hurting the other person. You should also show empathy at this point of the apology and acknowledge the damage caused to the other person. Without empathy, your apology will feel empty no matter what you say; always remember that.

- **Responsibility** means that you accept accountability for your actions. It means that you don't blame anyone for what happened, and neither are you making excuses. Instead, it is best to take full responsibility for your actions and the consequences.

- As you might have guessed, **Remedy** involves showing the willingness to take the necessary action to better the situation. The remedy part of the apology can involve a promise not to do it again, promising to work on yourself, stating how you will remedy the situation, or restituting the harm caused (if possible).

A Sample Apology for Being Emotionally Abusive

If you've been emotionally abusive, you could say something like:

"I am so sorry for emotionally abusing you. I can't even begin to imagine what this put you through. The anger you might have felt, the confusion, the doubt, the disappointment, I'm so sorry for all of it. I now realize the impact of my actions and how much I hurt you. If I ever made you feel like I acted as I did because of something you did or said, I'm so sorry; it was all my fault and caused by my own issues.

I promise that this will never happen again as I have realized what I have been doing, and I am consciously taking action to make sure that this never happens again."

TIP: If you have decided to seek professional help, include it in the apology; it will show your partner that you are truly committed to self-betterment and resolving "your issues."

Chapter 6: About Knowing Your Triggers (& False Beliefs)

As I talked to Josh that evening, I asked him why things had gotten so bad this time. He said he had no idea, that he had just lost control. I then knew that I was asking the wrong question, at which point I asked him what had happened. "What triggered the fight," I said.

First, he seemed to be in deep thought, as if he didn't know or didn't want to say. After nudging him a bit more, which I always do, he spoke up:

"Well, the whole of this week has been hectic. Martha has been especially busy, and I would come home to an empty house. I would call her, and she would still be at work, which I would understand. I mean, she was working, so why shouldn't I understand, right?"

"Right," I said.

"But I mean, she's my wife, and I barely got to see her the whole week. We had made plans to go out for dinner tonight, but she canceled around 6 PM. So when she came in at around 10, I just asked her if her job was more important, you know? I even told her to choose between her job and me, but I didn't mean it. So she got mad and told me that we had bills to pay, and she didn't see me do too much to get them paid. You know how much I have been struggling to keep my business afloat, right?"

"Right," I said again.

"So I just got furious, and after exchanging a few heated words, and before I knew it, I held Martha, threw her on the floor, and started kicking. I mean, I was so angry mainly because I felt like I was losing her, and we never got to spend any time together. If only she made time for us, I don't think I would have been that angry."

Even with the flawed statement of assigning blame to Martha for his actions, Josh had a real concern here: that they were drifting apart, which was his trigger.

Triggers are a crucial part of abusive tendencies, and if you are genuinely committed to self-betterment, you need to understand yours.

What Are Triggers?

We can consider triggers repressed or suppressed emotions of fear, anger, regret, insecurity, or resentment that, once activated, cause an automatic and usually intense reaction. These reactions can either be abuse—or experienced as abusive by your spouse.

When it comes to triggers that cause abusive behavior, you need to identify the specific actions, situations, or words that trigger such emotional reactions, thus ensuring you can anticipate them and manage them to avoid abusive behavior.

Where should you start? Below is a list of shared triggers in abusive partners:

- **Rejection or feeling ignored**: Like Josh, some people get triggered into being abusive by feeling rejected or ignored. The most common cause of this is childhood neglect or abandonment.

- **Envy:** Envy can also trigger other people such that when somebody close to them achieves or gets something good, they automatically feel bad about themselves. Being "the less-favored child" or having a parent that ignored their needs are the most common causes of envy.

- **Shame:** When some people face any critical, rejecting, critical, or disapproving treatment, it can trigger them into being abusive. That may be because they were heavily shamed as adolescents or children.

"We Should Both Feel Bad Together"

Individual triggers aside, why do triggers lead to abuse? Usually, an abusive partner will resort to abuse out of feeling bad about themselves. In this case, the abuse may be a way of fending off guilt or shame for something they have done. This can usually happen if your partner is usually cheery, accomplished, or well-liked, which was the case for my friend Pam.

Pam had a loving husband who was the CEO of a small tech company, and everybody loved him. Jim, her husband, was so happy that every time he would come home, he would come twittering and laughing and get all affectionate with Pam. You would think that this would make any woman happy, but it certainly didn't make Pam happy: it drove her crazy.

Pam would always get angry and say something terrible to him, which brought him down, which she was trying to achieve in the first place. But then Jim would look so confused and sad, and she would feel bad for saying whatever she did. Pam started to feel very guilty for it, but she felt like she needed to do it because she was not as cheery as Jim.

When she came to talk to me about it, I asked her why her husband's happiness bothered her so much. She said that she felt miserable, and she felt that her life had no purpose, yet she had an accomplished and always-jolly husband. Pam used to sell Tupperware online, but she didn't need the money; she just did it to pass the time.

So I suggested that she digs deep and find something that she wanted to do. Additionally, I suggested that to avoid that trigger, she could try calming techniques because it would be unfair to want Jim to change his happy personality. Meanwhile, I told her to stay off Jim's way until she had all her issues in order.

Pam started meditating and going to yoga classes, specifically to calm her mind. She slowly started feeling good about herself, and when she started giving yoga classes, she finally felt she had a purpose and could now bask in Jim's happiness.

Your Anger Journal

Like Pam, many people are unaware of their triggers and the feelings that lie within those triggers. Can you remember the journal I suggested you keep earlier? Now you need to keep an anger journal.

In this journal, keep a log of any abusive incident and ask yourself what made you respond the way you did. This journal can help you identify any false beliefs you might have and your triggers too.

Trigger Solution Suggestions for Different Types Of Abuse

Nobody wants to be in a draining relationship. We all want to feel loved and happy. Simply because you feel bad doesn't mean that you should both feel bad. You can consciously turn your feelings around by feeling good for and about your partner.

Here are suggestions for various types of abuse.

For Domination/Control

The most straightforward advice I can give you is to get some control in your life. The need to control your spouse possibly comes from not feeling in control of yourself.

Assess every aspect of your life and find out where the problem could be. For example, are you dealing with an alcohol/drug problem? Are you slacking at work? Do you have past baggage that you still haven't dealt with and that is weighing you down?

Criticism or Negativity

If you only notice what your partner does wrong and their inadequacies, try developing an attitude of gratitude. Do this:

- Before you sleep or early in the morning, think about the good things that happened that day or the previous day. If you are doing this in the morning, you can also think about the good things you are looking forward to that day. Being grateful can help you gain perspective, mainly because we tend to focus only on the negative.

- Come up with a minimum of three considerate, caring, or thoughtful things that your partner did towards you or someone you hold dear.

- Now come up with three reasons why you are grateful for your partner. For instance, you could say, "I am grateful he is sober," or "I am grateful that she still loves me."

If you do your best to feel this gratitude deep inside you, you will start seeing more of the good in your partner.

Arbitrary Expectations

Have unreasonable expectations from your partner means your focus is mainly on the other person instead of yourself. Here, you need to start paying more attention to your efforts and what you are not doing to make the relationship successful.

Yes, there are things your partner might or might not be doing to make your relationship successful. There's nothing wrong with communicating that with your partner, as long as you do it correctly. However, if you find that you solely focus on your partner's actions and never yours, then that is where the problem is.

Do your part, meet your expectations for the relationship, and focus on changing what hinders you from meeting your expectations.

Being Overly Possessive

You cannot own another person. The more closely you attempt to hold someone close to you, the more they will pull away; that's how it is. That means any effort you put into "owning" your partner is counterproductive. If you loosen your grip, you will pull your partner closer.

Letting go is not easy because it all comes down to control, and your need for control can make you feel that when you stop putting up possessive measures, your partner will slip away from you.

When you feel that, remind yourself that, like all other creatures, humans want freedom. We want to choose to be close to someone or not, and we don't want to feel forced when we don't feel like it.

Here are a few examples of possessive behavior:

- You keep telling your partner that they don't love you or they don't feel how you feel about them

- You keep asking your partner if they love you and keep telling them that you do with the expectation of them saying it back

- Insisting on hugging or kissing your partner when they are with other people or when they don't want to

- Wanting and insisting that you have sex when you sense or feel that your partner isn't in the mood

- Assuming that your partner doesn't want to have sex with you or doesn't love you

- Making your partner feel guilty for not wanting to have sex as much as you do

- Wanting to know what your partner is doing all the time

- Accusing your partner of unfaithfulness all the time with no solid evidence

- Being all over your partner at a gathering to ensure everyone knows they are with you

To stop this, try the following:

- When you feel yourself pulling at your partner in whatever situation, recognize it and restrain yourself. Recognizing it is simple; if whatever you are about to say or do sounds irrational, is not factual, and is something you constantly say or do because of your insecurities, don't say or do it. Instead, remind yourself that your partner responds negatively to this possessiveness. If you really want to hear your partner say that they love you, think about how they have shown you this recently; after all, actions speak louder than words.

- If you are usually the one to initiate sex and are unhappy because you feel that your lover doesn't initiate it or don't like having sex as much, commit to not initiating for a month. I know a month seems like a long time, but it might not last this long. The point here is to relieve your partner of any pressure they might be feeling towards the constant plight for sex. Trust me, within a few weeks, your partner will miss it and want it as bad as you do—we both know nothing flows as good as mutual, consensual sex.

As you apply these tactics, you also need to work on two

major things: your trust and self-esteem. These are the major issues why we tend to hold on to people too tightly. These issues can trace back to your childhood or past relationships, and as you deal with your past, trust and self-esteem are some of the core things you will have to work on to keep growing.

Chapter 7: Clear, Open Communication is The Key

The importance of good and clear communication in a relationship is not something you should underestimate, more so when the relationship has emotional abuse issues.

Can you remember the last abuse incident Josh and Martha had?

Martha had accused' Josh of not communicating about anything substantial. Also, remember I had mentioned that sometimes they could stay for a week without speaking. Well, Josh usually blew up after the silent treatment phase.

When Martha would try to talk to John about an issue they might have argued about, he would brush it off and say that he was late for something or that he wasn't feeling well at the moment.

As time went by, Martha got somewhat used to this, and she never really bothered trying to sort things out. When he went silent, she also went silent, and this became the norm. When Josh saw that Martha had also gone silent, this would bother him to his core. He would start overthinking, wondering what Martha was thinking. *Is she planning to leave me? Does she want a divorce? Has she given up on me?*

So when he broke the silence, he never did it politely. Instead, he would ambush Martha with all of his doubts, and Martha would shout back, not dismissing his doubts; in other words, it was a mess: a pointless mess that never solved anything.

Now:

Imagine how different things would be if Josh had just openly talked to Martha when she came to him to resolve their issues. Imagine if he had dealt with his insecurities or talked to Martha about them. Imagine if they had both sat down and talked about what was eating away at their relationship. If they had done that, things would have been different and better to some degree.

Sometimes we complicate things so much when an hour's talk could solve everything. Sometimes relationships break over something that partners could have discussed and solved in 30 minutes or less. That highlights the importance of good communication, especially in a relationship.

Here are some key things you should keep in mind:

Learn How To Express Yourself

Sometimes, when people cannot express how they feel, they may resort to unhealthy modes of 'communication' such as silent treatment, assigning blame, or straight-up abuse. But why do some people find it so hard to express themselves? Again I blame this on childhood experiences.

As I had mentioned earlier, Josh's parents were pros at silent treatment. They would go for months without speaking to each other, and so, in some way, Josh considered this normal, which is why he saw nothing wrong with shutting Martha out.

Learning how to express yourself as an adult may be a bit hard if it is not your 'normal,' but you have to do it if you want to save your relationship (or any other relationship).

Here is a mini-guide on how you can express yourself better to get your point around:

Gather your thoughts

It can be challenging to say what you want to say if you don't know what to say, get it? If you have trouble expressing yourself, gather your thoughts beforehand.

If you need to write what you intend to say beforehand so that you can rehearse, don't hesitate to do it. Knowing that you have something substantial to say will make it easier to face your partner.

Don't dwell too much on the past

Dwelling on history will lead you to where we are trying to stay away from, which is assigning blame.

When you keep saying things such as, "you remember when you said..." or "remember when you did..." you are solving nothing.

The trick here is to be result-oriented. What is the point of the conversation? What are you trying to achieve? Is whatever you are saying going to help you achieve this?

You should focus on expressing how you feel—or felt towards something your partner did—and how you want to move forward.

NOTE: Remember that if you are dealing with insecurities that you want to discuss with your partner, that's okay. However, remember that the only way to deal with these is from within.

There is little your partner can do about such issues, and to some point, it might be unfair to lay them down on them, yet there is nothing they can do about them.

Nevertheless, if you have real concerns, such as your partner sending too much time with an ex and others that touch on your insecurities, openly talk about it because your partner can do something about it.

Be clear and respectful

Insults and criticism will not get you far. Instead, remember the end goal you have attached to your conversation and assess whether criticism and insults will do anything to help you achieve this.

Beating around the bush can have you digging up things you don't want to be digging up at that moment. So the best approach is to be as direct and as clear as possible without throwing politeness out of the window.

For example, if you want to be spending more time with your partner say exactly that. It can be as simple as saying, "It would be amazing if we would spend more time together. Can we please put something on the calendar?" That's simple and direct.

If you lose your cool somewhere along the way, politely ask your partner to give you a break and return to the conversation when you have calmed down.

Learn how to compromise

You can't always have your way; your partner also has opinions and personal life; you have to be respectful. Therefore, work on understanding and emphasizing with your partner about any topic you are discussing.

If you find yourself pushing your point too hard while your partner is of another opinion, you've gone a bit too far, and you have to come back to compromise. The rule of thumb here is never to push it.

Listening

As you try to sharpen your communicating skills, listening can be as important as communicating. But, unfortunately, we often listen to reply instead of listening to understand.

You will need to teach yourself how to listen to what your partner is truly saying. If that means you won't have something to say when your partner finishes saying what she has to say, that is better than constantly thinking about what you will say as your partner talks.

Read your partner's body language, facial expressions, words, and listen to the entire conversation. After listening to your partner, paraphrase the conversation to ensure you understand it better yourself. Your partner can then confirm that what you rephrased is what they meant, and then from there, you can reply from a place of understanding.

Be keen on what bothers them the most. You can go ahead and ask your partner this directly. Whatever your partner tells you is what you should focus on working on first. When you do, your partner will feel heard, loved, and respected; this is how your partner should always feel in your relationship.

Conclusion

Congratulations, you have read to the end of this book, and oh, what a journey it was! I know that by now, you've learned and experienced all sorts of emotions that you never thought you would experience. I'm certain that by now, you are not the same as you were before and as you were reading this book.

We started by learning that you are not the only one to blame for your abuse; your childhood and experiences have a lot to do with this, and you are certainly not a bad person.

We then looked at how to look into your past to deal with the root cause of your abuse. We also learned how to keep anger and impulses in check and how to stop being abusive. We also went ahead and learned how to communicate effectively to avoid misunderstandings in relationships.

You can agree with me that we have exhaustively learned how to stop being abusive. As you continue to heal, refer to this book as much as you need to.

I wish you good luck!

PS: I'd like your feedback. If you are happy with this book, please leave a review on Amazon.

Please leave a review for this book on Amazon by visiting the page below:

https://amzn.to/2VMR5qr

Made in United States
North Haven, CT
30 October 2023

43413937R00046